Augsburg
Organ
Library

LENT

Augsburg Fortress
Minneapolis

Augsburg Organ Library: Lent

Edited by Norma Aamodt-Nelson, Christopher Sidorfsky, and Eric Vollen
Cover designed by Richard Krogstad
Music engraved by David Moklebust

The paper used in this publication meets the minimum requirements of American National Standard for Information Sciences—Permanence of Paper for Printed Materials, ANSI Z329.48-1984.

ISBN 0-8006-5897-3
AF 11-11036

04 03 02 01 00 1 2 3 4 5

CONTENTS

INTRODUCTION

The twentieth century witnessed a significant renewal of the organ and its music. Not only did the manner in which organs were built undergo substantial changes, but newly written music reflecting these changes flourished around the world. In fact, the organ experienced a revival that few in the nineteenth century could have predicted. The Augsburg Organ Library is a reflection of this profound renewal of the instrument and its music.

Following the rich romantic instruments of the late nineteenth and early twentieth centuries, European and North American organ builders alike revived classic principles of organ building mid-century through the influence of the *Orgelbewung* (organ revival movement). The resulting instruments were characterized by a warm singing tone, clarity of pitch, and responsive key action. By the end of the twentieth century, organ building had returned to its place as an art of the highest caliber.

Also during this time, organists and composers experienced a renewed interest in the classic forms and structures of the organ's earliest literature. The rediscovery and widespread distribution of a large corpus of organ works from composers of the sixteenth and seventeenth centuries led to a creative outburst among contemporary composers and organists. These musicians did not, however, simply reproduce the past. Older forms and structures, rather, were often wedded to newer melodic, harmonic, and rhythmic possibilities. The result was a century of compositions that invites both serious contemplation and regular performance.

The Augsburg Organ Library is a multi-volume collection that reflects this twentieth century renewal of the organ and its music. The compositions included in this series come from a variety of cultural and religious traditions. Music from England, Belgium, France, Germany, Scandinavia, and North America forms the basis of the library. As such, the variety of notational traditions and organ nomenclature has been retained in order to reflect original sources and performance practices. The result is a rich compendium of organ music that serves as a basic performing library for church organists.

Organized according to the church year, special focus has been placed on the seasons of Advent, Christmas, Epiphany, Lent, Easter, and November (the end times). A wide range of selections has been carefully chosen for each season of the church year. Music that primarily supports the song of the worshiping assembly is included; repertoire designed solely for concert or recital has been avoided. The majority of compositions are based on commonly used hymn tunes that are widely known in English-speaking countries.

A primary goal has been to include organ voluntaries (prelude, offertories, postludes, and so forth) that range from two to six minutes in length. Many of these compositions can also serve as extended introductions to congregational hymn singing. The level of difficulty ranges from medium-easy to medium-difficult. All compositions are playable on a two-manual organ with pedal.

Aberystwyth

Savior, When in Dust to You

Sw: Strings
Gt: Solo Flute
Ped: Bourdon 16', Sw/Ped

Gerald Near

Tune: Joseph Parry, 1841–1903
Arrangement: Copyright © 1967 Augsburg Publishing House

Augsburg Organ Library: Lent, ISBN 0-8006-5897-3

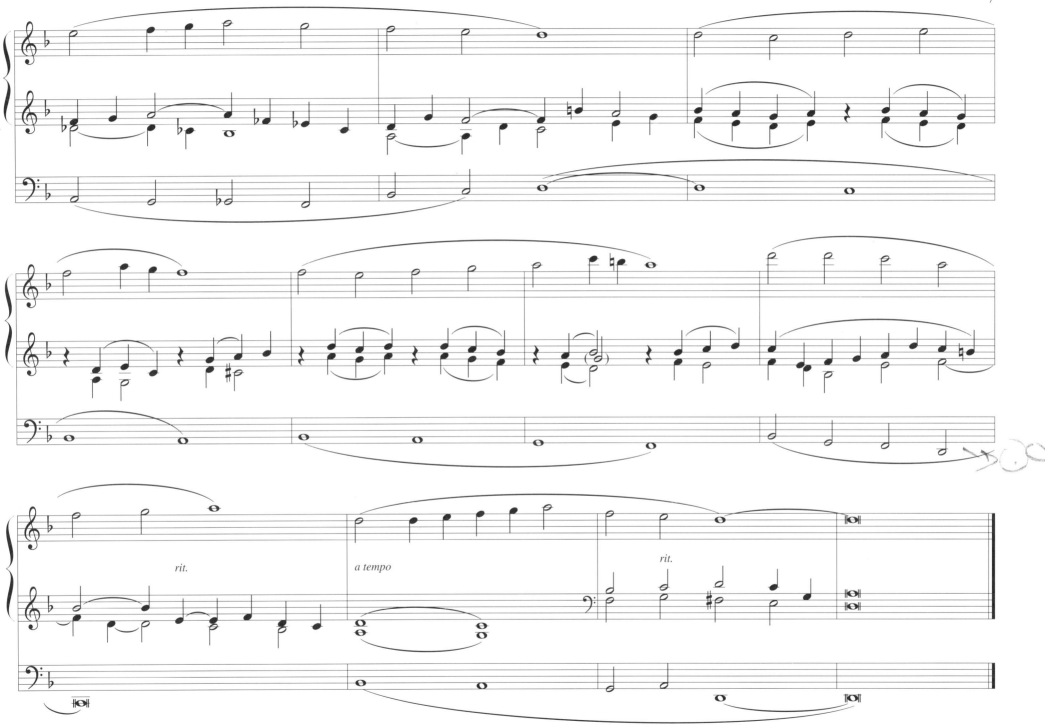

Aus tiefer Not

Out of the Depths I Cry to You

Max Drischner

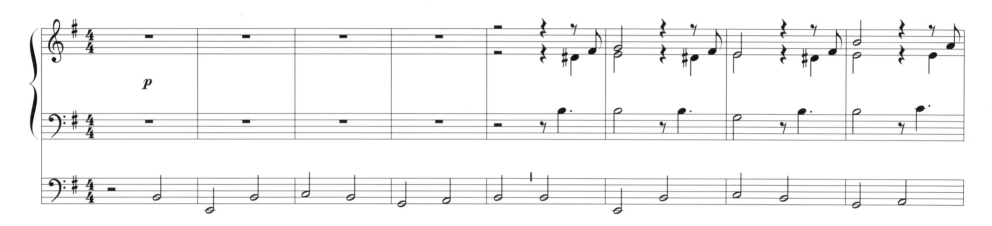

Tune: Martin Luther, 1483–1546
Arrangement: Copyright © 1918 C. L. Schultheiss Musikverlag, Tübingen

* Von hier an stufenweise steigern bis zum *ff*. Man kann auch den folgenden Teil auf 2 Manualen spielen.

II

Beach Spring

Wash, O God, Our Sons and Daughters

or

Lord, Whose Love in Humble Service

I

Wayne L. Wold

I: Principal 8'
II: Flute 4', Tremulant
III: Flutes & Strings 8'
Ped: Flutes 16', 8', III/Ped

Slowly, expressively, freely

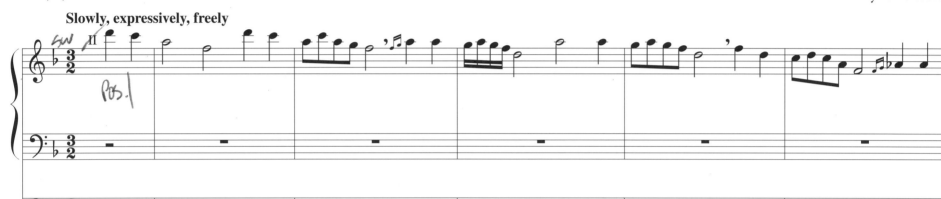

Tune: *The Sacred Harp,* 1844

Augsburg Organ Library: Lent, ISBN 0-8006-5897-3

Berglund
O Blessed Spring

I: 8', 2'
II: 8', 4'
Ped: Solo stop 4'

James Biery

Tune: Robert Buckley Farlee, copyright © 1993 Robert Buckley Farlee. Used by permission.
Arrangement: Copyright © 1996 Augsburg Fortress

Augsburg Organ Library: Lent, ISBN 0-8006-5897-3

Bred dina vida vingar
Thy Holy Wings

Sw: Strings 8'
Gt: Solo Flute
Ped: *mp* Solo 4'

Richard Webster

Tune: Swedish folk tune

Augsburg Organ Library: Lent, ISBN 0-8006-5897-3

Calvary

I: *mp*
II: *mf*
Ped: to balance Sw.

Richard Billingham

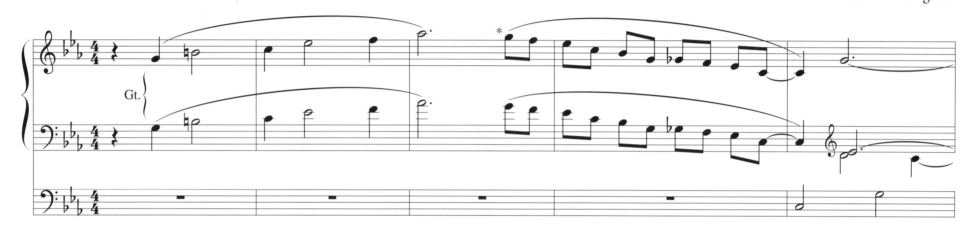

Tune: African American spiritual
Arrangement: Copyright © 1996 Augsburg Fortress

Augsburg Organ Library: Lent, ISBN 0-8006-5897-3

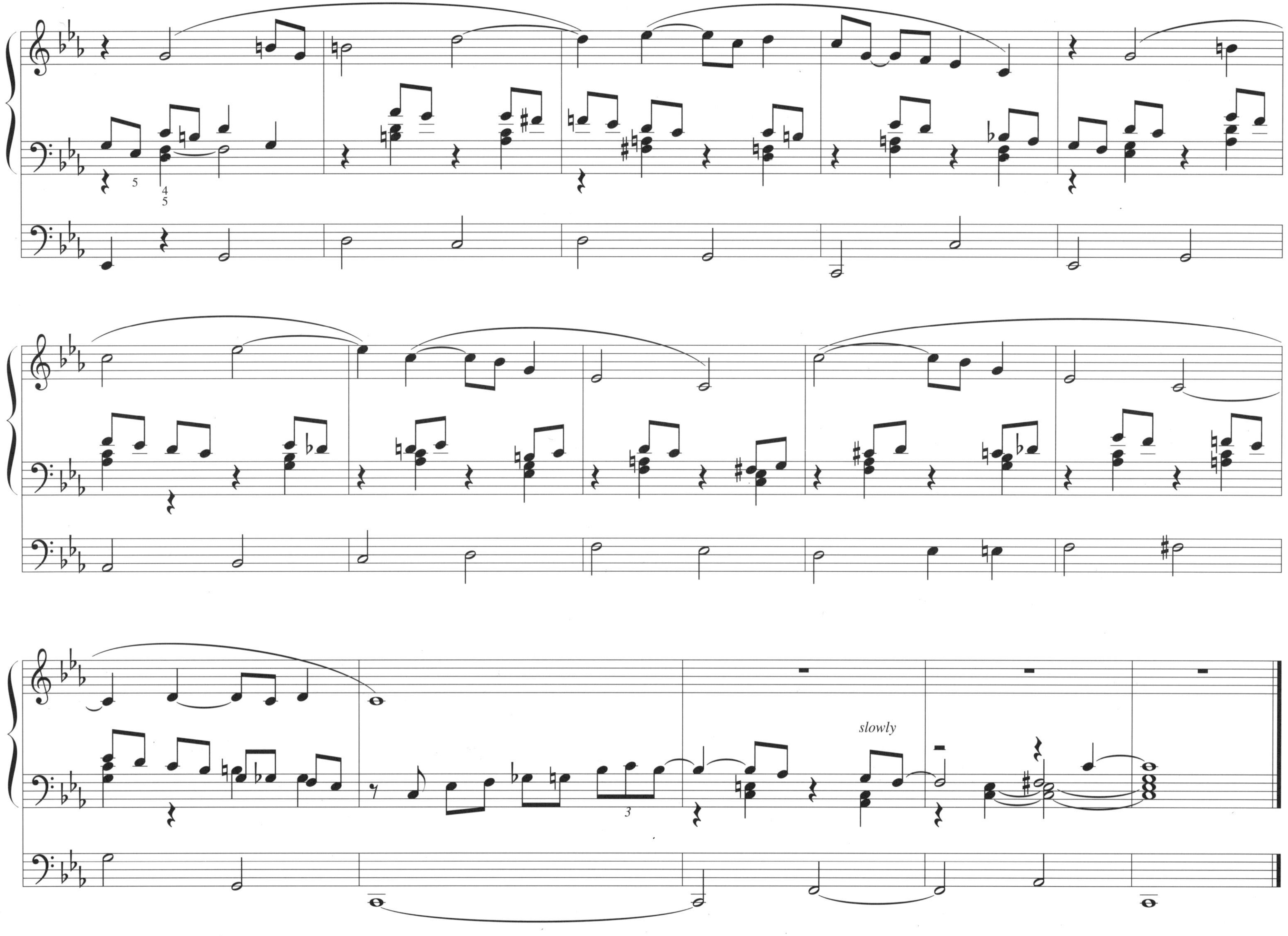
slowly

Choral Dorien

Réc: Fl. 8' et Gambe 8'
Pos: Cor de nuit et Salicional
G.O.: Fl. Harm.
Ped: Soubasse

Acc.
G.O./Réc
G.O./Pos
Pos/Réc
Tir/Pos et Réc

Jehan Alain

Lent et très lié

Réc. boite fermée

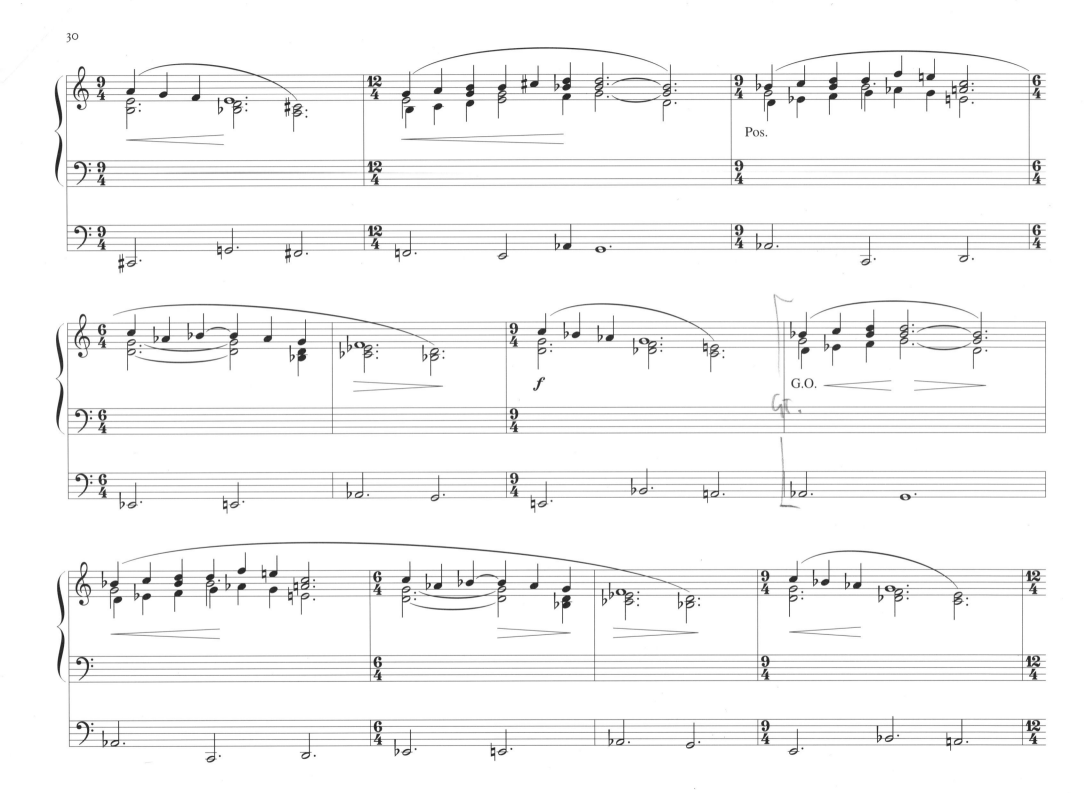

* Si la voix céleste est très douce, on pourra l'utiliser ici.

FSP P. 16 8F 8P   SW 8P   GT. 8P 8F

Consolator

Come, Ye Disconsolate

I: Flute or String ensemble *pp – mp*
II: Principal 8'; prepare 4', 2'
Ped: 32', 16' *pp*; prepare *mf*

J. Bert Carlson

Peacefully (♩ = 88)

Tune: Samuel Webb, 1740–1816

Augsburg Organ Library: Lent, ISBN 0-8006-5897-3

Ellacombe

Hosanna, Loud Hosanna

I: Solo Reed
II: Principals 8', 4', 2', Mixture
III: Flutes 8', 4', 2'
Ped: 16', 8', 4'

J. Wayne Kerr

Tune: *Gesangbuch der Herzogl. Wirtembergischen Katholischen Hofkapelle,* 1784
Arrangement: Copyright © 1998 Augsburg Fortress

Gethsemane
Go to Dark Gethsemane

I: Principals 8', 4', 2²/₃'; Flutes 8', 4'
II: Strings or Soft Flute 8'
Ped: 16', 8', 4'; I/Ped

David Cherwien

Tune: Richard Redhead, 1820–1901

Arrangement: Copyright © 1989 MorningStar Music Publishers of St. Louis. All rights reserved. Used by permission.

Healer of Our Every Ill

Sw: Flutes 8', 4'
 Gt: Flutes 8', 4', Sw/Gt
Ped: 16', 8'

Jeffrey Honoré

Tune: Marty Haugen, b. 1950; Copyright © 1987 GIA Publications, Inc. All rights reserved. Used by permission.

Herzlich tut mich verlangen

O Sacred Head, Now Wounded

Sw: Flute 8', Gambe 8', Celeste 8'
Ped: Octave 4' or Reed 4'

Pamela Decker

Espressivo e legatissimo (♩ = 63)

Tune: Hans Leo Hassler, 1564–1612
Arrangement: Copyright © 1997 Augsburg Fortress

Ped: change to Soft 16', 8'

Herzlich tut mich verlangen

O Sacred Head, Now Wounded

Sw: Flute 8'
Ped: Choralbass 4' or (soft reed 4')

Timothy Flynn

Tune: Hans Leo Hassler, 1564–1612
Arrangement: Copyright © 1991 Timothy Flynn. Used by permission.

Herzlich tut mich verlangen

O Sacred Head, Now Wounded

Anton Wilhelm Leupold

Tune: Hans Leo Hassler, 1564–1612

Augsburg Organ Library: Lent, ISBN 0-8006-5897-3

Herzliebster Jesu

Ah, Holy Jesus

Beverly A. Ward

Tune: Johann Crüger, 1598–1662
*Also quoting *Ecce iam noctis,* Sarum plainsong, Mode IV

52

54

Jesu, Kreuz, Leiden und Pein

Jesus, I Will Ponder Now

I: Oboe
II: Flute

Robert Below

Tune: Melchior Vulpius, c. 1560–1615
Arrangement: Copyright © 1993 Augsburg Fortress

Jesu, meines Lebens Leben

Christ, the Life of All the Living

II: Cromorne 8', Tierce 1³/₅'
III: Flutes 8', 2'
Ped: 16', 8'

Flor Peeters

Tune: *Das grosse Cantionale,* Darmstadt, 1687
Arrangement: Copyright © 1966 by C. F. Peters Corporation. Used by permission.

II: – Cromorne 8'
+ Flute 8', Nasard 2²/₃'

Love Unknown
My Song Is Love Unknown

I: Oboe
II: Soft Flute and Strings 8'
Ped: Soft 16', 8'

Karl Osterland

Tune: John Ireland; copyright © 1974 The John Ireland Trust. Used by permission.

Martyrdom
Alas! And Did My Savior Bleed

I: Flutes 8', 4'
II: Flutes 8', 2' (or Cornet V)
Ped: 16', 8'

Robert Buckley Farlee

Tune: Hugh Wilson, 1764–1824

Augsburg Organ Library: Lent, ISBN 0-8006-5897-3

New Britain

Amazing Grace, How Sweet the Sound

Philip Gehring

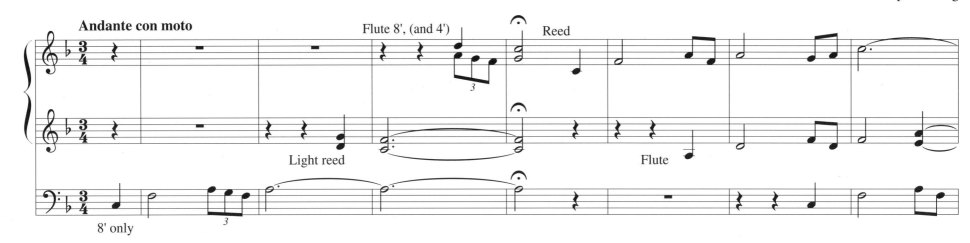

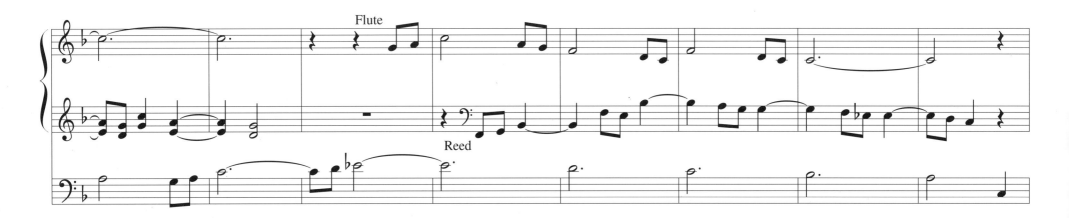

Tune: W. Walker, *Southern Harmony*, 1835
Arrangement: Copyright © 1972 Augsburg Publishing House

Augsburg Organ Library: Lent, ISBN 0-8006-5897-3

Olivet
My Faith Looks Up to Thee

I: Soft 8', 4'
II: Solo
Ped: Soft 16', 8'

Karl Osterland

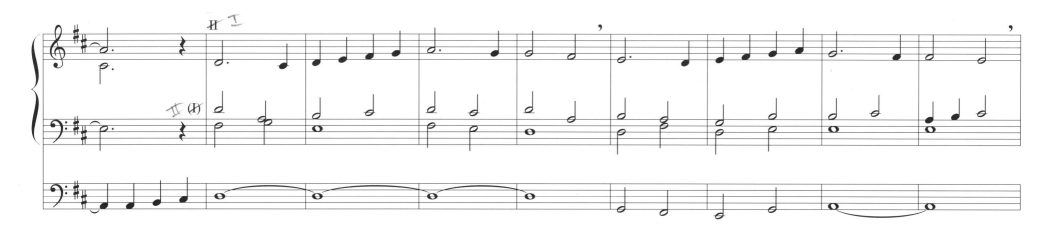

Tune: Lowell Mason, 1792–1872

Augsburg Organ Library: Lent, ISBN 0-8006-5897-3

O Welt, ich muss dich lassen

O Bread of Life from Heaven

G. Winston Cassler

Tune: (Innsbruck) Heinrich Isasc, c. 1450–1517
Arrangement: Copyright © 1975 Augsburg Publishing House

Augsburg Organ Library: Lent, ISBN 0-8006-5897-3

Pange lingua
Of the Glorious Body Telling

Sw: Strings
Ch: Soft Reed
Gt: Ch/Gt
Ped: Gemshorn 16', Flute 4'

Ronald Arnatt

Dedicated to Temple Dunn

Tune: Sarum Plainsong; mode III, Vatican collection
Arrangement: Copyright © 1968, 1986 Ronald Arnatt. Used by permission.

Sw. soft Flutes 8', 4'

Ch. soft Reed

+ 4'

rit. Sw. *ten.*

più **p** *allargando*

4' only

Rathbun
In the Cross of Christ I Glory

I: Full, II/I
II: Full with Reeds
Ped: Full, Reed 8', II/Ped

David Cherwien

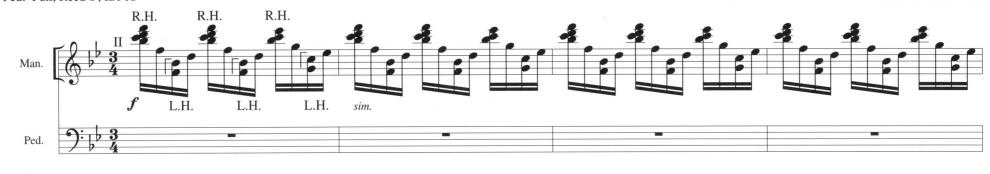

Tune: Ithamar Conkey, 1815–1867
Arrangement: Copyright © 1989 MorningStar Music Publishers of St. Louis. All rights reserved. Used by permission.

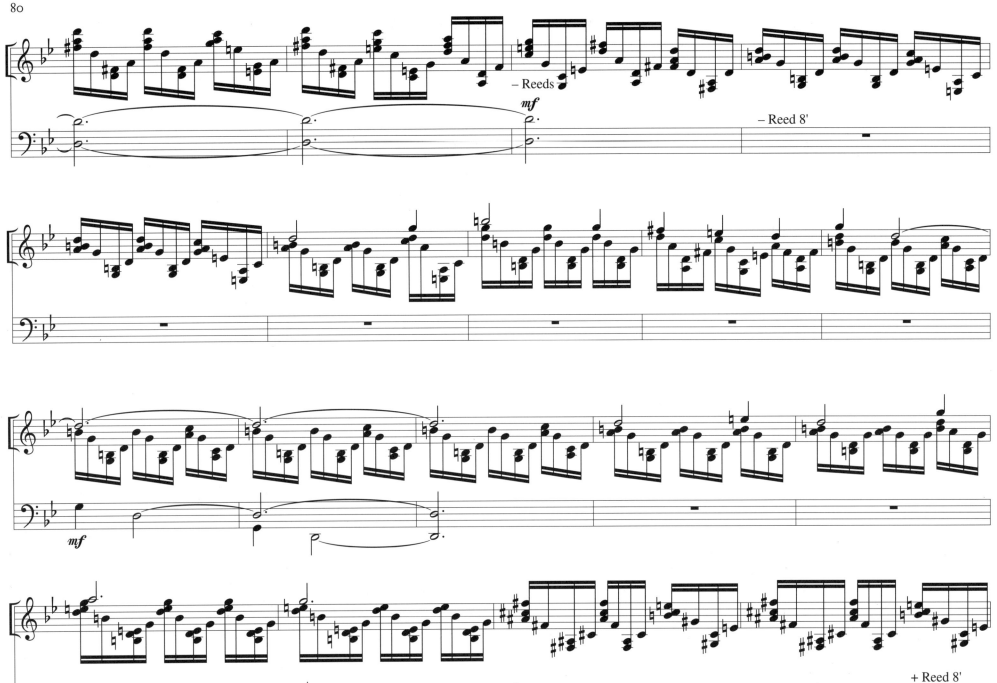

poco a poco cresc.

+ Reed 8'

+ Reeds 16'

+ Reeds 16'

ff Full Organ

+ 32', + I/Ped

Rhosymedre
My Song Is Love Unknown

Sw: Soft Flutes 8', 4'
Gt: (Stopped Diapason) 8'; Sw/Gt
Ped: Soft 16'; Sw/Ped

R. Vaughan Williams

Tune: John D. Edwards, 1806–1885

Augsburg Organ Library: Lent, ISBN 0-8006-5897-3

Rockingham Old

When I Survey the Wondrous Cross

I: Clarinet 8'
II: Strings (and Flutes) 8'
Ped: Soft 16', 8'

Robert Buckley Farlee

Tune: adapt. Edward Miller, 1731–1807

Augsburg Organ Library: Lent, ISBN 0-8006-5897-3

Seelenbräutigam
Jesus, Still Lead On

I: Krummhorn 8'
II: Flutes 8', 4' (or Strings)
Ped: 16', 8'

Paul Manz

Tune: Adam Drese, 1620–1701

Augsburg Organ Library: Lent, ISBN 0-8006-5897-3

Shades Mountain

There in God's Garden

Man: Flues 8', 4', (2')
Ped: Solo Trumpet 8'

Robert Buckley Farlee

Tune: K. Lee Scott; copyright © 1987 MorningStar Music Publishers of St. Louis. Used by permission.

rit.

– Reed
+ Flues 16', 8'

♩. = 80

c.f.

mf

cresc. poco a poco

f

Slane
Be Thou My Vision

Sw: Voix Celeste 8', Flutes 8', 4'
Gt: Krummhorn 8', trem.
Ped: Bourdon 16', Octave 8', Flute 8'

Franklin D. Ashdown

Molto legato e poco rubato ($\downarrow$ = 80-84)

Tune: Irish melody

Somewhat slower, poco rubato

Gt.

Krummhorn 8'

Sojourner
I Want Jesus to Walk with Me

Gt: Foundations 8'
Sw: Flute 4'
Ch: Clarinet
Ped: Soft 16', 8'

Raymond Henry

Tune: African American spiritual
Arrangement: Copyright © 1996 Augsburg Fortress

Prepare: Ped. Reed 4' as solo
Sw. Strings 8', 4'

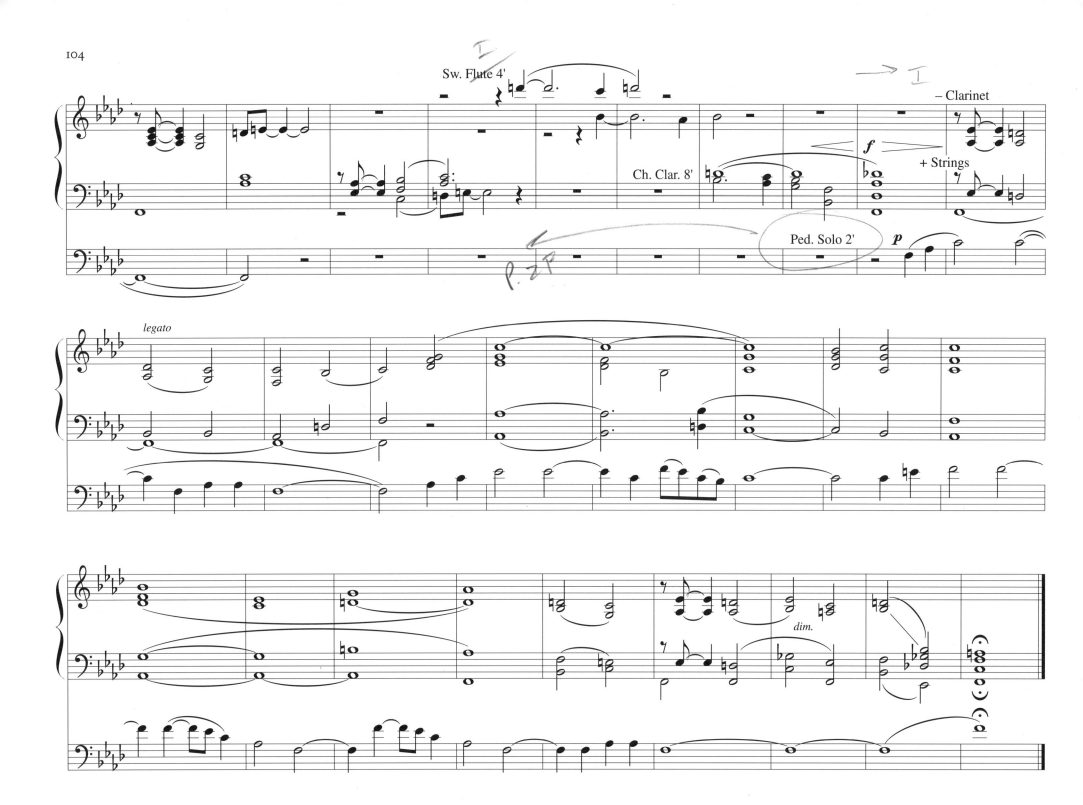

Song 1
Lord, Who the Night You Were Betrayed

Man: Flutes 8', 2', 1' (or 8', 4', 1¹/₃')
 Ped: Solo 8'

Robert Buckley Farlee

Tune: Orlando Gibbons, 1583–1625
Arrangement: Copyright © 1996 Augsburg Fortress

Southwell
Lord Jesus, Think on Me

I: Flute or Strings 8'
II: Reed 8'
III: Principals 8', 2'
Ped: Flutes 16', 8'

J. Bert Carlson

Tune: *Psalmes* by William Daman, 1579
Arrangement: Copyright © 1995 Augsburg Fortress

Augsburg Organ Library: Lent, ISBN 0-8006-5897-3

III

Left blank for ease of page turns.

Ubi caritas
Where True Love and Charity Are Found

Sw: Strings
Ped: Flute 8'

Marilyn Biery

Tune: Mode VI

Augsburg Organ Library: Lent, ISBN 0-8006-5897-3

Valet will ich dir geben

All Glory, Laud, and Honor

Emma Lou Diemer

Tune: Melchior Teschner, 1584–1635

Arrangement: Copyright © 1979 Augsburg Publishing House, admin. Augsburg Fortress

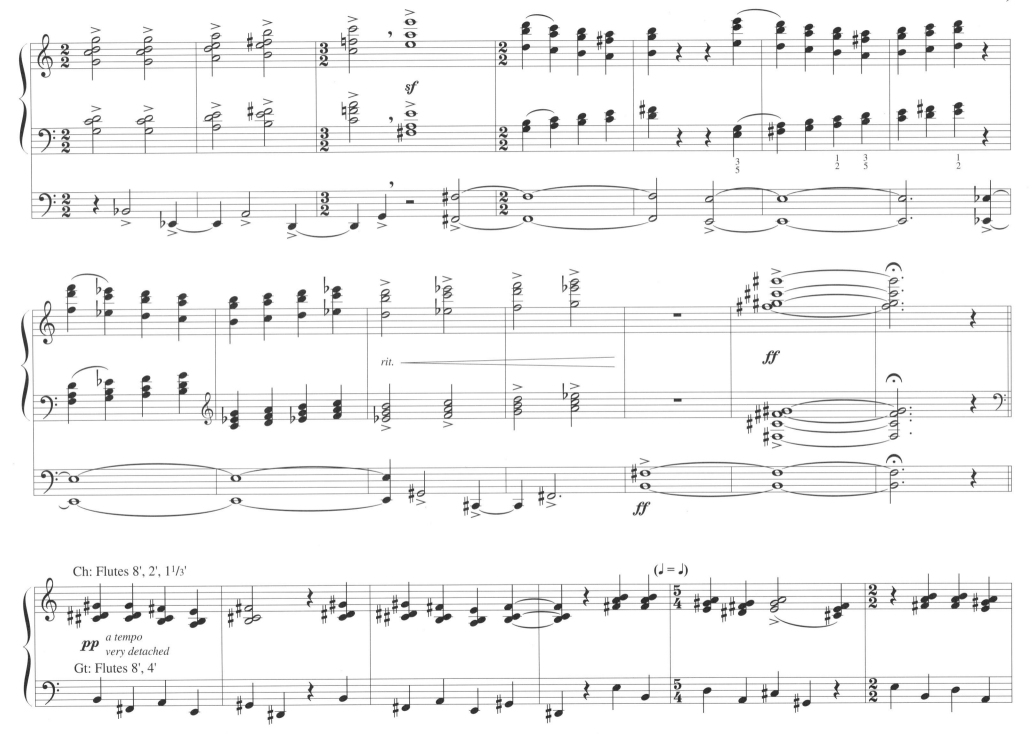

rit.

Sw.

a tempo

Flutes 8', 4', 2'

f

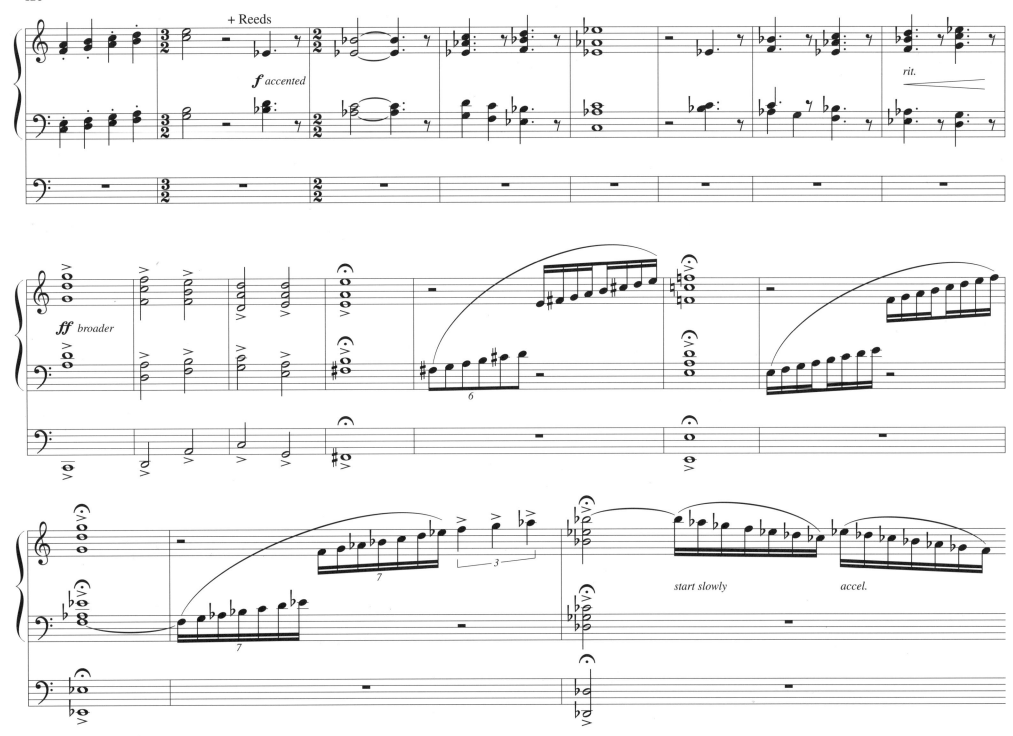

Were You There

Emma Lou Diemer

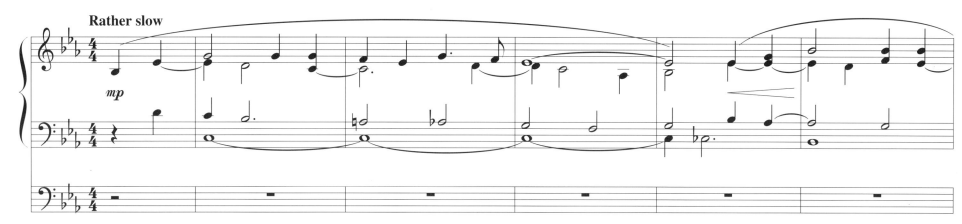

Tune: African American spiritual
Arrangement: Copyright © 1975 Augsburg Publishing House, admin. Augsburg Fortress

Augsburg Organ Library: Lent, ISBN 0-8006-5897-3

COMPOSERS

Jehan Alain (1911–1940)
Assistant Organist
St. Germain-en-Laye, France

Ronald Arnatt (b. 1930)
Organist and Director of Music and Arts,
Trinity College, Boston

Franklin D. Ashdown (b. 1942)
Freelance Composer and Physician
Organist and Choir Director, Church of Jesus Christ of
Latter Day Saints

Robert Below (b. 1934)
Professor of Music, Lawrence University,
Appleton, Wisconsin

James Biery (b. 1956)
Director of Music, Cathedral of St. Paul, St. Paul

Marilyn Biery (b. 1959)
Co-Choir Director and Organist,
Cathedral of St. Paul, St. Paul

Richard Billingham (b. 1934)
Associate Professor, University of Illinois, Chicago
Organist, First Methodist Church, Chicago

J. Bert Carlson (b. 1937)
Pastor, Christ Lutheran Church, Whiting, New Jersey

G. Winston Cassler (1906–1990)
Professor of Music
St. Olaf College, Northfield, Minnesota

David Cherwien (b. 1957)
Visiting Instructor of Music, Gustavus Adolphus College,
St. Peter, Minnesota
Director of Music Ministries,
Lutheran Church of the Good Shepherd, Minneapolis

Pamela Decker (b. 1955)
Assistant Professor of Organ and Music Theory
University of Arizona, Tucson

Emma Lou Diemer (b. 1927)
Professor of Composition and Theory
University of California, Santa Barbara

Max Drischner (1891–1971)
Organist-Kantor, Nikolaikirche, Brieg

Robert Buckley Farlee (b. 1950)
Associate Pastor and Director of Music,
Christ Church Lutheran, Minneapolis

Timothy Flynn (b. 1962)
Diocesan Music Consultant, Lansing, Michigan

Philip Gehring (b. 1925)
Professor, Valparaiso University, Valparaiso, Indiana

Raymond Henry (b. 1931)
Freelance Composer and Music Educator, New York
Accompanist, Concord Baptist Church, Brooklyn

Jeffrey Honoré (b. 1956)
Director of Liturgical Music,
St. Matthias Church, Milwaukee

J. Wayne Kerr (b. 1958)
Minister of Music,
First United Methodist Church, Hurst, Texas

Anton Wilhelm Leupold (1868–1940)
Organist, Petrikirche, Berlin

Paul Manz (b. 1919)
Professor and Artist in Residence Emeritus,
The Lutheran School of Theology at Chicago,
Christ Seminary-Seminex
Cantor Emeritus, The Evangelical Lutheran Church of
St. Luke, Chicago

Gerald Near (b. 1942)
Freelance Composer

Karl Osterland (b. 1956)
Church Musician, Historic Trinity Lutheran Church, Detroit

Flor Peeters (1903–1986)
Organist, St. Rombaut Cathedral, Melchelen, Belgium
Professor of Organ, Lemmens Institute

Beverly A. Ward (b. 1935)
Director of Music, St. James Episcopal Church,
Hendersonville, North Carolina

Richard Webster (b. 1952)
Organist and Choirmaster, St. Luke's Episcopal Cathedral,
Evanston, Illinois
Lecturer, Northwestern University
Music Director, Bach Week Festival

R. Vaughan Williams (1872–1958)
Professor of Composition,
Royal College of Music, London

Wayne L. Wold (b. 1954)
Associate Professor of Music and College Organist,
Hood College, Frederick, Maryland
Director of Chapel Music, Camp David,
Thurmont, Maryland

INDEX OF COMPOSERS

INDEX OF COMMON TITLES